TikTok Riches: Your Guide to Monetizing Your Creativity

Table of Content

Chapter 1: Understanding TikTok - A Platform Like No Other

The Origin Story: How TikTok Became a Social Media Sensation

It all started with short lip-sync videos on Musical.ly and the Chinese app Doujin. Fast forward a few years, and these platforms merged to form what we now know as TikTok. This chapter isn't just about dates and acquisitions; it's a story of how TikTok transformed from a niche app into a global powerhouse, changing the way we think about social media and entertainment.

The Power of 60 Seconds: Embracing Short-Form Video

Why has TikTok's format, often just 15 to 60 seconds, captivated millions? Here, we'll look at how TikTok mastered the art of short-form content, perfectly aligning with our decreasing attention spans and thirst for quick, digestible entertainment. It's a shift that has not only won over Gen Z but has also had us all - from teens to grandparents - scrolling for hours.

Who's Watching? Unpacking TikTok's Diverse Audience

Initially the realm of teens, TikTok's audience is now as varied as its content. This section delves into who is really watching and engaging with TikTok videos. We'll sift through the data and trends to reveal a platform that's as popular with millennials and older generations as it is with its Gen Z base.

Cracking the Code: The Magic Behind the Algorithm

One of TikTok's biggest mysteries is its algorithm. Why do some videos go viral overnight while others languish? This part of the chapter is like a detective story, uncovering the secrets of the "For You Page" and how it can make a creator's content go viral, regardless of their follower count.

Trendsetting on a Global Scale

TikTok isn't just where trends happen; it's where they're born. This section explores how dances, challenges, and memes start on TikTok and end up everywhere, shaping pop culture in a way no other platform has before.

The Rhythm of TikTok: Music as a Content Catalyst

Here, we delve into the heartbeat of TikTok: its music. We'll look at how a perfect soundtrack can turn a simple video into a viral sensation, and the nuances of navigating music rights and trends to make your content pop.

TikTok in the Social Media Universe

How does TikTok stand out in the crowded world of social media? This part compares TikTok with giants like Instagram and YouTube, pinpointing exactly what makes it unique and why it's become a favorite for creators worldwide.

Mastering TikTok's Toolbox

Finally, we'll get hands-on with TikTok's features. From basic editing to advanced effects, this section is a practical guide to using TikTok's creative tools to bring your vision to life.

In this opening chapter, we're setting the stage for your TikTok journey. It's a mix of storytelling, data-driven insights, and practical advice - a foundation that will help you understand not just the 'how' but the 'why' of TikTok's incredible rise. As we move forward, these insights will be your guide to navigating this dynamic platform, whether you're looking to entertain, influence, or monetize. Welcome to the world of TikTok, a place where creativity knows no bounds.

Chapter 2: Setting Up for Success on TikTok

Crafting Your TikTok Identity: More Than Just a Profile

Your TikTok journey begins with your profile. It's not just a digital placeholder; it's your personal brand's first impression. We'll talk about choosing the right username, creating an engaging bio, and selecting a profile picture that captures your essence. Your profile should tell a story at a glance – a story about who you are and what kind of content you create.

Finding Your Niche: The Key to Standing Out

In a sea of content, finding your niche is like finding your North Star. This section explores the importance of carving out your unique space on TikTok. Whether it's comedy, dance, education, or something entirely different, understanding and embracing your niche will guide your content creation and help you connect with the right audience.

Consistency is King: Building a Content Strategy

Randomly posting videos is like shooting arrows in the dark. This chapter emphasizes the importance of a consistent content strategy. We'll discuss how often to post, the best times to do so, and how to keep your content fresh yet true to your brand. A well-thought-out strategy not only keeps your audience engaged but also helps you stay on track with your creative goals.

Unleashing Creativity Within Constraints

TikTok's time constraints aren't a limitation; they're a canvas for creativity. Learn how to tell compelling stories, share valuable information, or simply entertain, all within the span of a minute or less. This part includes tips and tricks for maximizing impact while keeping within time limits.

The First Impression: Crafting Your Debut Content

Your first few TikToks can set the tone for your journey on the platform. We'll guide you through planning and creating your debut content, ensuring it aligns with your identified niche and appeals to your target audience.

Engaging with Trends (Without Losing Your Uniqueness)

Trends are a driving force on TikTok, but jumping on every bandwagon isn't the answer. This section focuses on how to engage with trends smartly and creatively, ensuring that while you stay relevant, you also retain your unique voice and style.

Collaborations: Growing Together

Collaborating with other TikTokers can be a game-changer. It's not just about reaching a wider audience; it's about community and co-creation. We'll discuss how to choose the right collaborators and create content that's mutually beneficial and engaging.

Aesthetic and Style: The Visual Language of Your Content

Finally, we'll talk about the importance of aesthetics and visual consistency. Your videos should have a recognizable style, whether it's through your use of color, filters, or editing techniques. A consistent aesthetic helps in building a brand identity that's instantly recognizable.

Chapter 2 is your blueprint for getting started on TikTok. From crafting a captivating profile to creating content that resonates with your target audience, this chapter provides the tools and insights necessary to build a solid foundation on the platform. As you turn these pages, you're not just setting up a TikTok account; you're crafting a digital persona that will resonate with millions of potential followers. Welcome to the exciting first steps of your TikTok journey!

Chapter 3: Content Creation and Strategy on TikTok

Understanding the TikTok Content Landscape

TikTok is a melting pot of content styles and genres. This section sets the stage by providing an overview of the types of content that thrive on TikTok. From dance videos to comedy sketches, from DIY tutorials to heartfelt stories, we'll explore the diverse content landscape of the platform, helping you identify where your creativity fits in.

Mastering the Art of TikTok Storytelling

In the world of TikTok, storytelling is an art form. Despite the time constraint, effective storytelling can captivate and engage your audience. This part of the chapter will guide you through the process of creating compelling narratives, whether you're sharing a personal story, presenting a product, or just having fun.

Utilizing TikTok's Unique Features and Tools

TikTok offers a plethora of features and tools that can enhance your content. Here, you'll learn how to use filters, effects, and music to their fullest potential. We'll also delve into the latest features TikTok has introduced and how they can be creatively incorporated into your content strategy.

Creating a Content Calendar: Organizing Your Creative Process

Consistency is key on TikTok, but it shouldn't come at the cost of quality. This section focuses on developing a content calendar that balances regular posting with ample time for creativity and production. You'll learn how to plan your content in advance, ensuring a steady stream of quality videos.

Engaging with Your Audience: Beyond Just Posting Videos

Engagement on TikTok doesn't stop at uploading videos. This part discusses the importance of interacting with your audience through comments, duets, and other community features. Engaging with your followers can build a loyal community and increase your content's reach.

Experimentation and Adaptation: Finding What Works Best

TikTok is constantly evolving, and so should your content. This section encourages experimentation with different content types, styles, and posting schedules to see what resonates most with your audience. It also covers how to use TikTok's analytics to inform your content strategy.

Creating Content with Virality in Mind

While there's no guaranteed formula for virality, certain elements can increase your chances. This part of the chapter explores tactics and strategies that can help your content go viral, including leveraging trends, using popular music, and creating relatable, shareable content.

The Ethics of Content Creation: Staying True to Yourself and Your Audience

As a content creator, it's important to maintain authenticity and adhere to ethical standards. This section addresses the importance of honesty and integrity in your content, including being transparent about sponsorships and avoiding misleading or harmful content.

In Chapter 3, we dive deep into the heart of TikTok: content creation. This chapter is designed to equip you with the skills, knowledge, and strategies to produce engaging, creative, and authentic content that resonates with your audience. Whether you're a budding creator or looking to refine your existing approach, this chapter will serve as your comprehensive guide to mastering the art of TikTok content creation.

Chapter 4: Building and Engaging Your Audience on TikTok

Laying the Foundation: Growing Your TikTok Following

This journey starts with understanding how to organically grow your following on TikTok. It's not just about numbers; it's about building a community of engaged viewers who resonate with your content. We'll explore strategies for attracting and retaining followers, including optimizing your content for discoverability and connecting with your audience on a personal level.

The Power of Engagement: Interacting with Your Audience

Engagement is the currency of TikTok. This section delves into the art of engaging with your audience through comments, challenges, and TikTok's duet feature. We'll discuss how authentic interaction not only boosts your visibility but also fosters a sense of community around your content.

Creating a Buzz: Leveraging TikTok Live Sessions

Live sessions on TikTok offer a unique opportunity to connect with your audience in real-time. This part of the chapter guides you through hosting successful live sessions, from planning the content to engaging with viewers during the live. We'll also cover best practices for promoting your live sessions to maximize attendance.

Collaboration: Expanding Your Reach

Collaborating with other TikTok creators can be a powerful way to expand your reach and tap into new audiences. Here, we'll explore how to identify potential collaborators, reach out for collaborations, and create content that benefits both parties.

Utilizing Hashtags and Trends for Visibility

Hashtags and trends are vital tools for increasing the visibility of your content on TikTok. This section provides insight into researching and using relevant hashtags, as well as participating in trends in a way that aligns with your brand and content style.

Handling Feedback: The Good, the Bad, and the Constructive

Receiving and handling feedback is an inevitable part of being a content creator. We'll discuss how to sift through comments, dealing with negative feedback constructively, and using positive and constructive criticism to improve your content.

Consistency and Adaptability: The Balancing Act

Consistency in posting is key to keeping your audience engaged, but so is adaptability. This part of the chapter focuses on striking a balance between maintaining a consistent posting schedule and being adaptable to changes in trends, audience preferences, and the TikTok platform itself.

Building a Brand, Not Just a Following

Ultimately, your goal on TikTok should be to build a brand, not just a following. This section ties together all the aspects of audience building and engagement, emphasizing how to create a brand presence that is authentic, relatable, and sustainable in the long term.

Chapter 4 is dedicated to the crucial aspect of audience building and engagement on TikTok. It covers everything from the basics of growing your following to the intricacies of engaging with your audience and building a personal brand. By the end of this chapter, you will be equipped with a comprehensive understanding of how to cultivate an active, loyal community around your TikTok presence.

Chapter 5: Monetization Strategies on TikTok

Introduction to Monetizing Your TikTok Presence

Monetization on TikTok isn't just about making quick cash; it's about strategically leveraging your presence for sustained financial success. This chapter introduces the various avenues through which TikTok creators can monetize their content and influence.

Navigating the TikTok Creator Fund

The TikTok Creator Fund is a direct way for creators to earn money from their content. We'll delve into the eligibility criteria, application process, and tips for maximizing your earnings through the fund. This section will help you understand how to turn your TikTok views and engagement into tangible income.

Brand Partnerships and Sponsored Content

Collaborating with brands can be a lucrative aspect of TikTok monetization. This section covers how to attract and secure partnerships with brands, craft successful sponsored content, and maintain authenticity while promoting products or services.

Affiliate Marketing on TikTok

Affiliate marketing is another avenue for monetization. We'll explore how to integrate affiliate marketing into your content strategy, choose the right products or services to promote, and effectively use affiliate links in your TikTok videos.

Selling Merchandise and Personal Products

For creators with a dedicated following, selling branded merchandise or personal products can be a significant income stream. This part of the chapter discusses how to design, promote, and sell your products through TikTok, including tips on e-commerce integration and fulfillment.

Utilizing TikTok to Drive Traffic to Other Platforms

TikTok can be a powerful tool for driving traffic to other platforms where monetization opportunities might be broader, such as YouTube, Instagram, or a personal blog. We'll discuss strategies for cross-promotion and converting your TikTok audience into followers and customers on other platforms.

Building a Personal Brand: Beyond TikTok

Your personal brand is your most valuable asset. This section emphasizes the importance of building a brand that transcends TikTok. We'll cover how to use your TikTok success as a springboard for other ventures, such as speaking engagements, book deals, or product lines.

Staying Compliant: Understanding TikTok's Monetization Policies

Monetizing on TikTok comes with the responsibility of understanding and adhering to the platform's policies. This section provides crucial information on TikTok's guidelines for monetized content, ensuring you stay compliant and avoid any potential pitfalls.

Chapter 5 provides a comprehensive guide to monetizing your TikTok presence. From participating in the TikTok Creator Fund to exploring brand partnerships and beyond, this chapter equips you with the knowledge and strategies needed to turn your TikTok success into a sustainable income source. By the end of this chapter, you'll have a clear understanding of the multiple paths to monetization on TikTok and how to navigate them effectively.

Chapter 6: Leveraging TikTok for Business Growth

Embracing TikTok in Your Business Strategy

TikTok isn't just for individual creators; it's a potent tool for businesses too. This chapter begins with an overview of how businesses of all sizes can utilize TikTok for marketing, branding, and audience engagement. We'll discuss why TikTok should be a part of your digital marketing strategy and how it can complement your other social media efforts.

Understanding TikTok's Business Audience

Unlike other platforms, TikTok's business audience is unique in its engagement and behavior. This section delves into the demographics and psychographics of TikTok users from a business perspective, helping you tailor your content to meet the expectations and interests of this audience.

Creating Business Content That Resonates on TikTok

What kind of content works for businesses on TikTok? This part of the chapter focuses on creating engaging, informative, and entertaining content that aligns with your brand identity while appealing to the TikTok audience. We'll cover different content types, from product showcases to behind-the-scenes glimpses, and how to present them creatively on TikTok.

Successful Campaigns: Case Studies of Brands on TikTok

Learning from successful examples is crucial. This section will showcase a series of case studies highlighting businesses that have effectively used TikTok to boost their brand presence, increase engagement, and drive sales. We'll analyze what made these campaigns successful and how you can apply similar strategies to your business.

Influencer Partnerships: Collaborating for Mutual Benefit

Partnering with TikTok influencers can significantly amplify your business's reach. Here, we'll explore how to identify the right influencers for your brand, establish successful collaborations, and measure the impact of these partnerships.

TikTok Ads: Navigating Paid Advertising on the Platform

TikTok's advertising platform offers businesses a range of options to promote their products or services. This part of the chapter will guide you through setting up TikTok ads, understanding different ad formats, targeting the right audience, and optimizing your ad campaigns for maximum ROI.

Measuring Success: Analytics and ROI on TikTok

How do you know if your TikTok strategy is working? We'll discuss the importance of TikTok analytics, what metrics to focus on, and how to use this data to refine your strategy and demonstrate ROI.

Building a Community Around Your Brand on TikTok

Finally, this chapter emphasizes the importance of building a community, not just a customer base, on TikTok. We'll provide tips on fostering a sense of community among your TikTok followers, encouraging user-generated content, and creating a brand persona that resonates with the TikTok audience.

In Chapter 6, businesses will find a treasure trove of insights and strategies on leveraging TikTok for brand growth and customer engagement. From content creation to influencer partnerships and paid advertising, this chapter serves as a comprehensive guide for businesses looking to harness the power of TikTok in their marketing efforts. By the end of this chapter, you'll be equipped with the tools and knowledge to effectively integrate TikTok into your business's digital marketing strategy.

Chapter 7: Navigating Challenges and Staying Compliant on TikTok

Understanding TikTok's Community Guidelines and Policies

Navigating the world of TikTok means understanding its rules. This chapter kicks off with an overview of TikTok's community guidelines and policies. Knowing these guidelines is crucial for creating content that is not only engaging but also compliant, ensuring your account remains in good standing.

Handling Negative Feedback and Online Criticism

Dealing with negative feedback is an inevitable part of being visible on social media. This section offers strategies for managing criticism in a constructive manner. We'll discuss the importance of maintaining professionalism, identifying constructive feedback, and dealing with trolls or inappropriate comments.

Ensuring Authenticity and Transparency in Your Content

As you grow on TikTok, maintaining authenticity becomes increasingly important. This part of the chapter emphasizes the need for honesty in your content, especially when dealing with sponsorships and brand deals. We'll cover how to disclose partnerships and maintain trust with your audience.

Respecting Copyright and Intellectual Property on TikTok

Understanding copyright laws is essential for TikTok creators, especially when using music, video clips, or other copyrighted material. This section provides guidance on how to respect intellectual property rights and avoid copyright infringement in your TikTok content.

The Ethics of Content Creation: Avoiding Misinformation and Harmful Content

TikTok, like any platform, can be a breeding ground for misinformation. This part of the chapter delves into the ethics of content creation, focusing on the responsibility of creators to avoid spreading false information and ensuring that their content is not harmful or misleading.

Managing Privacy and Security on TikTok

As your presence on TikTok grows, so does the importance of managing your privacy and security. We'll discuss best practices for protecting your personal information, dealing with hacking or phishing attempts, and ensuring your account's security.

Navigating Algorithm Changes and Platform Updates

TikTok's algorithm and features are constantly evolving. This section offers tips on staying adaptable and responsive to these changes, ensuring that your content strategy remains effective even as the platform evolves.

Creating a Sustainable and Responsible TikTok Presence

The final part of this chapter focuses on building a sustainable presence on TikTok. It's about finding a balance between pursuing growth and maintaining your wellbeing, along with a positive, responsible approach to content creation.

Chapter 7 is designed to equip you with the knowledge and tools to navigate the challenges of being a TikTok creator. From understanding and adhering to community guidelines to managing negative feedback and respecting copyright, this chapter provides a comprehensive guide to maintaining a responsible and compliant presence on TikTok. By the end of this chapter, you'll be prepared to face the challenges of the platform while keeping your integrity and authenticity intact.

Chapter 8: Analytics and Growth Tracking on TikTok

Demystifying TikTok Analytics: A Comprehensive Guide

Understanding TikTok analytics is crucial for measuring the success and impact of your content. This chapter begins by breaking down TikTok's analytics dashboard, explaining metrics like views, engagement rates, follower growth, and more. You'll learn how to interpret these metrics and use them to refine your content strategy.

Setting and Measuring Goals: What Success Looks Like for You

Success on TikTok can mean different things for different creators. This section helps you set clear, achievable goals, whether they're related to follower count, engagement rates, brand partnerships, or personal milestones. We'll discuss how to measure your progress towards these goals using TikTok's analytics tools.

Analyzing Your Audience: Who's Watching and Engaging?

Knowing your audience is key to content success. This part of the chapter dives into TikTok's audience insights, showing you how to analyze your followers' demographics, interests, and behaviors. Understanding your audience helps tailor your content to their preferences, leading to better engagement and growth.

Content Performance Analysis: Understanding What Works

What makes a TikTok video successful? Here, we'll explore how to analyze the performance of your content. By examining your most and least successful videos, you'll gain insights into content trends, optimal posting times, and elements that resonate with your audience.

Adjusting Your Strategy Based on Data

Analytics aren't just numbers; they're a roadmap for strategy refinement. This section emphasizes the importance of using analytics data to adapt and evolve your content strategy. Whether it's tweaking your posting schedule, experimenting with new content types, or focusing on particular topics, data-driven decisions can significantly impact your TikTok success.

Competitive Analysis: Learning from Others

Understanding what works for others can inform your own strategy. This part of the chapter covers how to conduct a competitive analysis, examining what successful TikTok creators in your niche are doing right and how you can apply similar tactics or identify gaps in their strategies.

Long-Term Growth: Building a Sustainable TikTok Presence

Short-term viral hits are great, but long-term growth is the goal. This section discusses how to use analytics for sustainable growth, focusing on long-term trends in your content's performance and audience engagement.

Utilizing External Tools for Enhanced Analytics

Finally, we'll look at external tools and resources that can complement TikTok's native analytics. These tools offer deeper insights and can be particularly useful for advanced creators or businesses looking to maximize their TikTok presence.

Chapter 8 is your guide to mastering TikTok analytics and using data to grow your presence on the platform. From understanding the basics of TikTok's analytics dashboard to setting goals and refining your strategy based on data, this chapter provides the knowledge and tools you need to track your growth and achieve success on TikTok. By leveraging these insights, you can make informed decisions that propel your TikTok journey forward.

Chapter 9: Beyond TikTok - Diversifying Your Presence

The Importance of a Multi-Platform Strategy

TikTok might be your launching pad, but it shouldn't be your only destination. This chapter begins by highlighting the importance of diversifying your online presence. We'll discuss the benefits of extending your reach to other social media platforms, like Instagram, YouTube, and Twitter, and how they can complement and enhance your TikTok success.

Cross-Platform Promotion: Expanding Your Digital Footprint

Successfully managing your presence across multiple platforms can significantly amplify your influence. This section offers strategies for cross-promotion, such as leveraging your TikTok content on other platforms and encouraging your TikTok audience to follow you elsewhere. We'll also cover how to tailor your content to suit the different formats and audiences of each platform.

Using TikTok Success as a Springboard

Many TikTok creators have leveraged their platform success to launch careers in other fields. This part of the chapter explores how you can use your TikTok visibility as a springboard into areas like acting, music, podcasting, or entrepreneurship. We'll include inspirational stories of TikTokers who have successfully transitioned into other ventures.

Creating a Cohesive Brand Across All Platforms

While each social media platform has its unique characteristics, maintaining a cohesive brand across all your channels is crucial. This section covers how to ensure consistency in your messaging, aesthetics, and content across different platforms, reinforcing your brand identity and making it easily recognizable.

Engaging with Different Audiences on Different Platforms

The audience on TikTok may differ significantly from those on other platforms. Here, we delve into understanding and engaging with these different audiences effectively. We'll discuss how to adapt your content and engagement strategies to meet the expectations and preferences of each platform's user base.

Navigating the Challenges of a Multi-Platform Presence

Managing multiple social media accounts comes with its own set of challenges. This section offers practical advice on dealing with these challenges, including time management, content planning, and dealing with platform-specific issues.

Monetizing Your Presence Across Platforms

Diversification also means more opportunities for monetization. We'll explore various ways to monetize your presence on different platforms, from sponsored content and advertisements to merchandise sales and exclusive content on platforms like Patreon.

Building a Long-Term Digital Strategy

Finally, this chapter concludes with insights into developing a long-term strategy for your digital presence. We'll cover how to stay adaptable and relevant in the ever-changing social media landscape, ensuring your online career is not just a fleeting success but a sustainable and evolving journey.

Chapter 9 equips you with the strategies and insights needed to expand your presence beyond TikTok and establish a robust, multi-faceted digital persona. By diversifying your platforms, you can maximize your reach, engage with a broader audience, and open up new avenues for personal and professional growth. This chapter is your guide to building a successful, enduring brand in the digital world.

Conclusion: Embracing the Future of Digital Content Creation with TikTok

The Ever-Evolving Landscape of TikTok

As we conclude this journey through "TikTok Riches," it's important to recognize that TikTok, like the digital world at large, is continuously evolving. The strategies, insights, and tips outlined in this book provide a foundation, but the key to sustained success on TikTok lies in staying adaptable, creative, and responsive to the platform's ever-changing nature.

The Power of Community and Creativity

TikTok has underscored the immense power of community and creativity in the digital age. Whether you're a creator, a business, or a brand, the platform offers a unique opportunity to connect with audiences in authentic, innovative, and engaging ways. The success stories and strategies discussed in this book highlight the potential of TikTok not just as a social media platform, but as a cultural phenomenon.

Monetization: A Byproduct of Passion and Consistency

While monetization is a significant focus of this book, it's crucial to remember that financial success on TikTok is often a byproduct of passion, consistency, and genuine engagement with your audience. The most successful TikTokers are those who stay true to their unique voice and content, building an authentic connection with their followers.

The Future of TikTok and Digital Content

Looking ahead, TikTok is poised to remain at the forefront of the social media landscape. Its impact on music, culture, and even politics is a testament to its reach and influence. As a creator, staying informed about trends, platform updates, and emerging features will be key to leveraging TikTok's potential in the future.

A Final Word of Encouragement

For those embarking on their TikTok journey, this book is just the beginning. The path to success on TikTok is as diverse as the platform itself. With creativity, adaptability, and a willingness to explore and experiment, the possibilities are limitless.

Embracing Change and New Opportunities

As you continue to grow and evolve on TikTok, be open to change and new opportunities. The digital world offers endless possibilities for those willing to explore and innovate. Your TikTok journey might start with a single video, but where it leads is up to you.